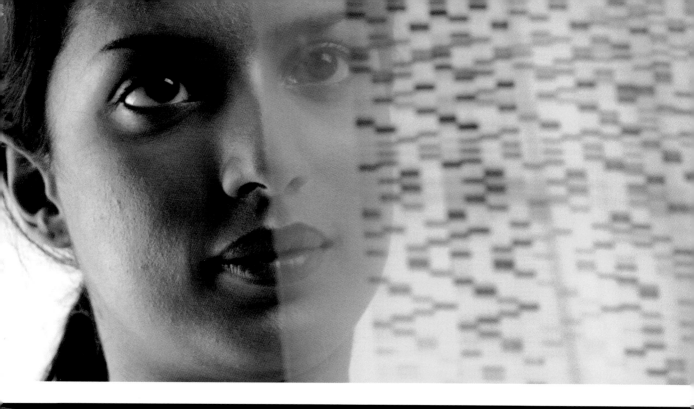

CUTTING EDGE MEDICINE

Genetics in Medicine

Andrew Solway

W
FRANKLIN WATTS
LONDON • SYDNEY

First published in 2007 by
Franklin Watts
338 Euston Road
London NW1 3BH

Franklin Watts Australia
Hachette Children's Books
Level 17/207 Kent St, Sydney, NSW 2000

Produced by Arcturus Publishing Limited,
26/27 Bickels Yard, 151–153 Bermondsey Street, London SE1 3HA

Editor: Alex Woolf
Designer: Nick Phipps
Consultant: Dr Eleanor Clarke

Picture credits:
Rex: 52 (Sunset)
Science Photo Library: 5 (Bluestone), 7 (Pasieka), 8 (D. Phillips), 10 (A. Barrington Brown),
13 (Tim Vernon, LTH NHS Trust), 15 (Laguna Design), 17 (Eye of Science), 18 (ISM),
21 (Laguna Design), 22 (J. C. Revy, ISM), 25 (Volker Steger), 27 (Eye of Science), 28 (Pascal
Goetgheluck), 31 (Pascal Goetgheluck), 32 (David Scharf), 35 (P. Plailly/Eurelios), 36 (Gary
Parker), 39 (P. Plailly/Eurelios), 40 (James King-Holmes), 43 (Hybrid Medical Animation),
45 (Geoff Tompkinson), 47 (Andrew Leonard), 48 (Antonia Reeve), 50 (Pasquale Sorrentino),
54 (Professors P. Motta and T. Naguro), 57 (David Parker), 58 (Bluestone).

Every attempt has been made to clear copyright. Should there be any inadvertent omission,
please apply to the publisher for rectification.

A CIP catalogue record for this book is available from the British Library

Dewey Decimal Classification Number: 616'.042

ISBN: 978 0 7496 6969 0

Printed in China

Contents

CHAPTER 1

What is Genetics?

Genetics is the science of heredity – the similarities and differences that pass between generations (from parents to offspring) of humans, other animals, and plants. Genetics involves the study of genes, the tiny biological blueprints of life, that make us human or grow an oak tree from an acorn. The fascinating science of genetics includes research into how genes work and what controls them, the discovery of the links between genetics and diseases, and how we use genetic information to understand and improve our quality of life.

Genetics is a fairly young science, less than two hundred years old, but one that has become a powerful tool in medicine. We have also created clones – exact genetic copies – of many existing plants or animals using genetic techniques. Thanks to our knowledge of genetics, we may one day be able to grow entire human organs to replace those that are failing, damaged or genetically faulty.

Yet while genetics holds great promise for medicine in the future, it also raises many troubling questions. Is it right to select the genes of an unborn child in order to create a 'designer baby' with a desired body shape, eye colour or level of intelligence? What will

CUTTING EDGE — SCIENCE

What is a cell?

A cell is the smallest complete unit of a living organism. Every cell is a highly organized structure within a definite border – either a cell membrane (in animals) or a cell wall (in plants) – that includes the cytoplasm, or main body of the cell, and a 'command centre', or nucleus. The nucleus also contains a complete copy of that organism's genetic information.

All living things are made up of cells. Micro-organisms, such as bacteria, are single cells. An adult human, on the other hand, contains about 100 trillion cells. The nucleus of nearly every human cell contains a dark material called chromatin, which forms into rod-shaped structures called chromosomes during cell division. Each chromosome contains hundreds of genes.

happen if we come to depend on herds of cloned animals for food? How will our ability to predict what diseases people might get or how long they will live affect our everyday lives? What safety precautions are in place to prevent genes from one species accidentally transferring to another species? Perhaps the biggest question of all is: who decides where we draw the line concerning the use of genetic procedures?

A great grandmother (right) with her daughter, granddaughter and great-granddaughter. All four have many genes in common.

What are genes?

Genes are what make every living thing look and behave as it does. All the genes in a cell or organism are collectively known as a genome. We receive our genes from our parents. But how exactly are genes passed on from one generation to the next? What information do they carry, and how do they carry it?

DNA, chromosomes and genes

Every cell in your body (except for mature red blood cells) holds within it the key to your genetic information, or genome. Most of the time, this genetic material is present in the cell's nucleus as an unordered substance called chromatin. When the cell begins to divide, however, the chromatin assembles itself into doubled strands called chromosomes. These chromosomes are made of long, twisted molecules of deoxyribonucleic acid (DNA). Definite, orderly sections of the DNA are called genes. Each gene contains hundreds of linked subunits known as nucleotides.

CUTTING EDGE   MOMENTS

Counting chromosomes

Chromosomes are hard to study because they only show clearly when a cell is dividing. In 1956, Swedish geneticists Joe Hin Tjio and Albert Levan found a way to 'freeze' cell division at a certain point and then separate the chromosomes. They were the first scientists to accurately count the number of chromosomes in human cells – 46.

Each nucleotide, in turn, consists of three parts: a sugar molecule, a chemical called a phosphate group and a chemical called a base. There are four bases – adenine (A), thymine (T), cytosine (C) and guanine (G) – and they link only two specific ways: A always links to T, and C always links to G.

In order to understand how the nucleotide sections join up to form genes, we need to go back to the idea of the twisted ladder structure of the DNA molecule itself. A pair of bases (A–T or C–G) connects to form the horizontal 'rung' of the DNA ladder, while the sugar molecule and phosphate group link to form the two sides that make up the 'backbone' of the DNA ladder. A designated section of

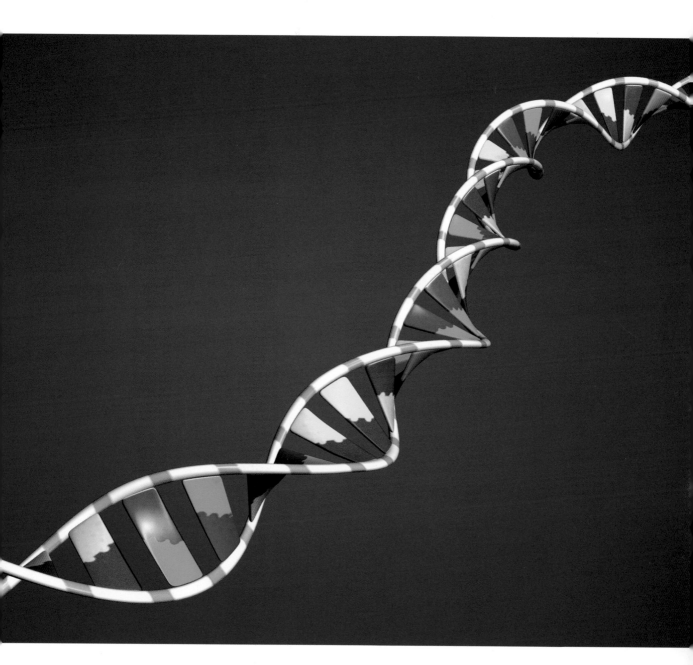

the DNA ladder with a specific arrangement of the bases is considered a gene. On average, each gene is about three thousand of these nucleotide subunits long.

Like the body cells themselves, DNA molecules have mastered the mathematical trick of multiplying by dividing. During a series of steps called mitosis (normal cell division), each chromosomal strand of DNA in the original 'parent' cell splits apart down the middle of its 'rungs'.

A simplified model of part of a DNA molecule. The two white and orange strips indicate the sugar-phosphate backbone, while the red, blue, green and yellow shapes are the base pairs.

Free bases in the nucleus pair with their complement, which results in a duplicate copy of the original chromosomal strand. The copied strand now contains a set of genes identical to those found on the original chromosome. As the parent cell continues its division of the nucleus and cytoplasm, one full set of 46 chromosomes – complete with all the genetic instructions (DNA) for that organism – moves into the nucleus within each new cell.

A micrograph (a photo taken using a microscope) of human sperm cells surrounding an egg cell. Only one sperm will fertilize the egg.

A different type of cell division, called meiosis, produces cells involved with human reproduction – female egg cells and male sperm cells, or gametes. Meiosis includes a second cell division that

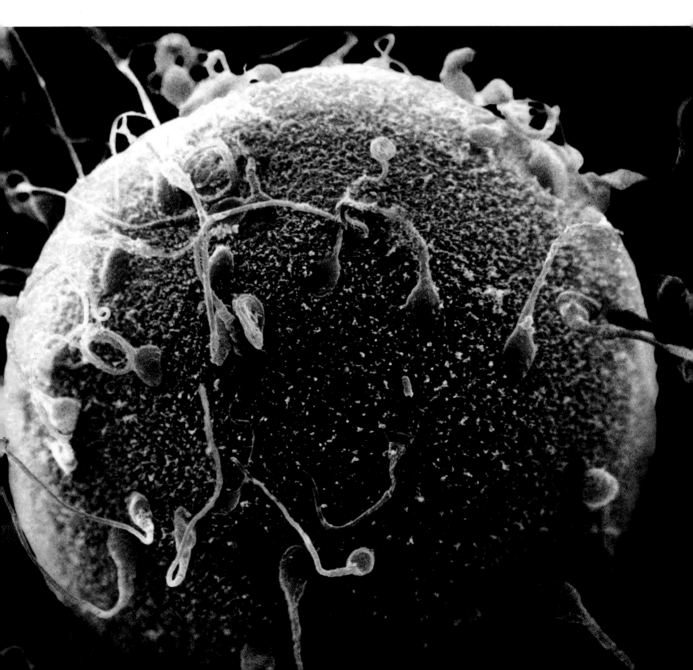

produces cells with only 23 chromosomes, half the normal number of chromosomes found in regular body cells. While meiosis follows the same basic replication steps as mitosis, in meiotic cell division, when the chromosomes split to replicate, they also exchange some genes. Two new cells form. Cell division continues in the new cells, and each pair of chromosomes then splits again, but they do not replicate. Instead, single chromosomes end up in each of the four new cells that form. These new cells contain only half the genetic information (DNA) of the original parent cell.

CUTTING EDGE SCIENCE

Giant molecules

A molecule is a collection of different atoms joined together. Some substances have small molecules made of just a few atoms. Water molecules, for instance, contain just three atoms. Many substances found in living things have much bigger molecules, made up of hundreds or thousands of atoms. DNA molecules are truly enormous. They can contain millions or even billions of atoms.

Specks of life

Human egg cells measure about a tenth of a millimetre across, while sperm cells are much smaller – about five microns (millionths of a metre) long. When these two tiny specks unite, a new life begins. Each gamete contributes half of the genes (and, therefore, half the DNA) needed to form a completely new human. The sperm cell contains genes (DNA) from the father, and the egg cell carries genes (DNA) from the mother.

During sexual reproduction, the father's sperm cells pass into the mother's body, and an egg and sperm meet to combine their genetic information. In this way, genes from each parent pass from one generation (the parents) to the next (the offspring). It only takes one sperm cell to combine with, or fertilize, an egg cell. This fertilized cell is the first cell of what will become a human being. While still small and growing inside its mother, this mass of cells is known as an embryo.

The embryo grows through many stages of cell division. After the embryo reaches a certain size, it is considered a fetus, which grows into a baby.

James Watson (left) and Francis Crick with their model of the DNA molecule.

Genes and proteins

The genes that make up our chromosomes carry information about how to make proteins. A protein molecule is a long chain of smaller units called amino acids, linked end to end. There are 20 different amino acids.

Genes carry instructions for the order of the amino acids in each protein chain. Even a small change in the arrangement of amino acids in a protein can prevent that protein from doing its job. The order of base pairs of the DNA in the gene is a code that the cell 'reads' to make a particular protein.

Proteins have two major functions in the body. Firstly, they make up most of the structure of certain body parts such as muscles. Secondly, proteins control metabolism – the processes going on in the body, such as helping us to digest our food.

CUTTING EDGE MOMENTS

Watson, Crick, Franklin and Wilkins

The discovery of the structure of DNA was made in 1953 by four people – James Watson, Francis Crick, Rosalind Franklin and Maurice Wilkins. X-ray 'pictures' of DNA taken by Franklin and Wilkins gave vital information about the shape of the DNA molecule and its size. But it was Watson and Crick, working in Cambridge, who worked out the final details of DNA structure using a large 3-D 'modelling kit'.

Making a protein

Proteins are not made in the nucleus, where all the cell's genetic material is kept. They are made in small structures called ribosomes, which are in the main part of the cell. The instructions for making a particular protein are carried from the nucleus to the ribosome by a special 'messenger' substance called messenger ribonucleic acid, or mRNA. RNA is similar to DNA, but it has slightly different nucleotides and it has only one chain, rather than two. Messenger RNA is one of several types of RNA. Like the genes in the nucleus, mRNA carries the protein instructions in the orderly arrangement of base pairs along its length.

In the main part of the cell the mRNA links up with a ribosome. The ribosome uses the coded information along the mRNA to make a protein, one amino acid at a time.

CHAPTER 2

From Genes to Characteristics

We know that genes are made of DNA, and they contain the information for making proteins. But how does this account for everything that genes do? Genes make us what we are. They control how a fertilized egg grows into a human baby, rather than a kitten or an oak sapling. Genes are also the reason for many of the differences between people. If someone has blue eyes and blond hair, these characteristics come from the person's genes.

Genes produce all these effects through proteins. Our eye colour and hair colour, for instance, depend on chemicals called pigments. Proteins called enzymes control the processes that produce these pigments.

Different genes

Over 99.9 percent of genes are the same in all humans. These are the genes that make us all human beings. The other 0.1 percent of genes are the ones that make us different from each other. For instance, six genes produce proteins that affect eye colour. Not everyone has the same version of each of these genes. Different versions of the same gene are known as alleles. Depending on which alleles a person has, his or her eyes can be any colour from light grey to dark brown.

CUTTING EDGE — FACTS

Human DNA

- Human DNA consists of 23 pairs of chromosomes. This amounts to around 3 billion subunits.
- There is about 1 metre of coiled-up DNA in every cell. If all the DNA in your body were stretched out, it would reach to the Sun and back about 650 times.
- About 97 percent of human DNA is long stretches of repeating sequences of bases that are not part of any gene.
- Current estimates are that human DNA contains about 30,000 genes. Scientists have identified about half of them.

Two of everything

The genes that you have are known as your genotype, and your physical characteristics, such as eye colour, height and nose shape, are examples of your phenotype. In the example of eye colour above it is fairly easy to see how the proteins produced by a gene can affect a characteristic. But it is not always so easy to understand how a person's genotype affects his or her phenotype.

One complication that makes it hard to understand the effects of a gene is that we have two copies of each gene. Humans have 23 pairs of chromosomes. One chromosome in each pair comes from the father, and one from the mother. The genes on a pair of chromosomes are for the same characteristics, but they may be different alleles. We will see some of the effects of this in the next chapter.

This computer artwork shows a chromosome (left) and a person with brown eyes. The highlighted area on the chromosome and the letters of genetic code next to it are supposed to represent the gene for eye colour. Two genes known to affect eye colour are found on chromosome 15, and one on chromosome 19.

Genes on and off

Some genes are essential to all cells, and are active most of the time. For instance, the genes that make the proteins involved in producing energy in the cell are active most of the time. However, most genes are only active at certain times, or in certain cells. For example, in young red blood cells, the genes for the protein haemoglobin (which carries oxygen in the blood) are switched on most of the time. By contrast, in hair cells in the skin, the genes for haemoglobin are turned off, but the genes for the protein keratin (the protein that hair is made from) are switched on.

We have two copies of every gene. How do they work together to give us our physical characteristics? In the 19th century, a Czech monk named Gregor Mendel discovered what became the basic rules for genetic inheritance. He knew nothing about DNA or genes, but he knew a lot about plants.

CUTTING EDGE SCIENTISTS

Gregor Mendel (1822–1884)

Gregor Mendel began training as a monk at St Thomas's monastery in what is now Brno, Czech Republic, when he was 21. He was interested in the sciences, especially botany, and in his mid-twenties he spent two years at university in Vienna, studying natural sciences (biology) and maths. In his work on peas, Mendel was trying to understand why crossing two kinds of plant can result in offspring that are especially strong and vigorous, but then the offspring of these vigorous plants do not have the qualities of their parents. Mendel's work did not solve this problem, but it did begin the science of genetics.

Mendelian genetics

Mendel spent many years studying how pea plants inherited different characteristics. He conducted thousands of experiments. For example, Mendel bred together a pea plant with purple flowers and one with white flowers. The plants that grew from this combination were all the same – they had purple flowers. Mendel then took these plants and bred them together. The next generation (the offspring of these plants) contained a mixture of white- and purple-flowered plants, which appeared in a consistent ratio – three purple-flowered plants to every one white-flowered plant.

Modern explanations

The ideas that Mendel suggested to explain these results formed the basis of modern genetics. He proposed that the parent plants each contribute one 'unit of inheritance' (what we now call a gene) to their offspring for each characteristic. But, he said, in any pair of characteristics, one of the two is dominant while the other is recessive. A dominant characteristic, or trait, is one that shows up

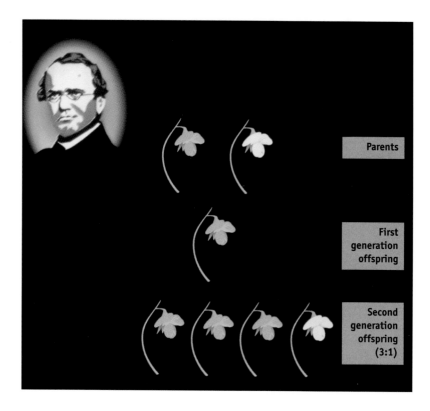

With his experiment on pea-plant flowers, Gregor Mendel showed that one gene could be dominant over another. When a white- and a purple-flower pea plant were bred together, all the offspring had purple flowers, because the purple-flower gene was dominant. However, the white-flower gene was not lost – it appeared again in the next generation.

physically, even when it is inherited only from one parent. A recessive trait cannot show unless it is inherited from both parents.

Today, we know that dominant and recessive characteristics are different alleles (types) of the same gene. In Mendel's pea plant experiment, the purple-flower allele was the dominant one, while the white flower was recessive. In the first part of the experiment, the purple-flowered plants had two purple-flower alleles (let's label them PP), while the white-flowered plants had two white-flower alleles (pp). The offspring had one allele from each parent – their genotype was Pp. Their phenotype, however, did not show evidence of the white-flower allele, because the purple-flower allele was dominant.

Mendel also concluded that it was a matter of chance as to which allele a parent passed on to its offspring. We can see how this works in the second part of Mendel's experiment. Each first-generation plant had two possible alleles: purple flower (P) or white flower (p). From the table on the right, you can see that there are four possible combinations of these two alleles. Three combinations produce purple flowers (PP, Pp, pP), but one combination (pp) produces white flowers. Since Mendel found experimentally that he grew three purple flowers for every one white flower, this suggests that there are equal chances for each combination of alleles to occur.

Not always so simple

Mendel devised some clear rules about inheritance of simple, contrasting characteristics, such as purple and white flowers. Not all characteristics are inherited in such a simple way, however. For instance, one allele is not always dominant over another. Snapdragons can have red flowers or white flowers, but they can also have pink flowers. Pink-flower snapdragons have one white-flower allele and one red-flower allele. Neither of the two alleles is dominant.

The biggest complication of inheritance in humans is that hardly any characteristics are inherited through a single gene. Eye colour,

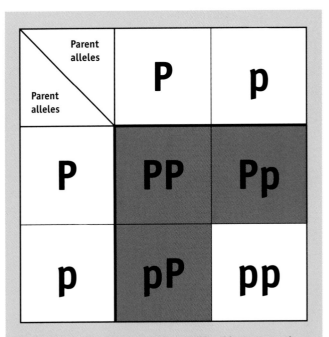

The upper row and left-hand column of this table represent the different alleles of the parent plants. The four boxes in the lower right-hand area represent the possible combinations of the parent alleles in the offspring. The purple-shaded boxes show which combinations produce purple flowers, and the white box shows which combination produces white flowers.

CUTTING EDGE — SCIENCE

Errors in DNA replication

Every time a cell divides, all the genetic material in the nucleus is copied. DNA is well designed to copy itself. The two strands of the DNA molecule 'unzip' from each other, and a new partner-strand is formed on each of the single strands. DNA replication (copying) is a mostly error-free process, but even so there is a copying error in every three or four cell divisions. If a copying error gets into a gamete, it will be passed on to the next generation. Usually the error will result in a defective gene, which may cause disease or death. But occasionally an error can give an advantage, such as immunity to (the ability to resist) a disease.

for example, involves at least six different genes. Other characteristics, for instance height, are the result of the interaction of many genes.

It is important to point out here that our characteristics and behaviour are not only affected by genetics. The environment and our upbringing are influential, too. For instance, a person's height is strongly affected by what his or her mother eats during pregnancy, and how well the person eats as a child.

Fruit flies are widely used for genetic research because they have unusual DNA in their salivary glands – the genes can be seen as dark and light bands. A copying error in the DNA of this fruit fly caused it to grow two pairs of wings instead of one.

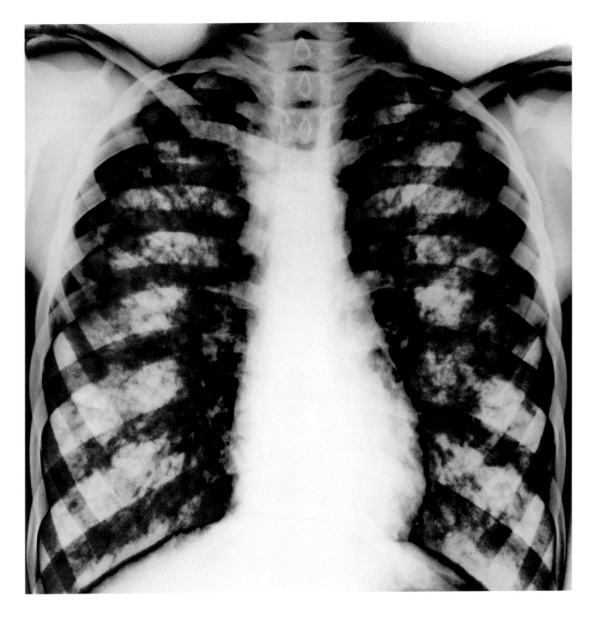

Genotype versus phenotype

In 1990, the Human Genome Project began. Its goal was to determine the sequence (order) of the whole human genome. This mammoth task was completed in 2003. As a result, we now know the order of all three billion base pairs in human DNA. Genes that hold codes for proteins make up only about two percent of the sequence; the rest is 'junk' DNA that does not code for proteins. Scientists know what about half of the 30,000 or so genes do, but it will take many years to find out what every gene does.

A coloured X-ray of the chest of someone with cystic fibrosis. The darker blue colour in the X-ray shows the thick mucus build-up caused by the disease.

Introducing variety

In humans, the only characteristics that have been found to be controlled by a single gene are certain hereditary or genetic disorders (disorders that are passed on through the genes from one generation to the next). Hereditary disorders can be caused when there is a mistake in the copying of the DNA in gametes (sex cells), and a gene is changed in some way. They can also be caused by mutations. Mutations are changes in the genetic material, often caused by outside factors such as exposure to ultraviolet light or other kinds of radiation.

Changes to the DNA usually cause problems that make a living thing less fit and healthy. However, some changes are beneficial. For instance, one mutation found in humans causes a particular protein to be missing from the surface of their cells. People with this mutation do not get the serious disease HIV/AIDS. Beneficial changes like this are responsible for the many differences between people, and ultimately for the huge variety of life on Earth.

CUTTING EDGE   FACTS

Some common genetic disorders

These are just a few of the 10,000 or so known genetic disorders:

Alzheimer's disease A brain disorder that causes people to slowly lose their memory and their ability to write or even speak. The disease most commonly affects elderly people.

Cystic fibrosis A disease in which thick, sticky mucus clogs up the lungs and digestive tract.

Duchenne muscular dystrophy and Becker muscular dystrophy Types of muscle-wasting disease.

Haemophilia A and B Blood disorders that prevent the blood from clotting properly, so that the slightest cut can cause serious bleeding.

Phenylketonuria One of the most common inherited disorders. It causes serious brain damage if not identified. Babies are tested for the disease at birth. If they have the disorder they are given a diet low in protein that allows them to live normally.

Sickle cell syndrome A blood cell disorder caused by an error in the structure of haemoglobin (the protein that carries oxygen in the blood). It affects the shape of the red blood cells and causes them to carry oxygen around the body less efficiently than in healthy people. It can also cause blood clots.

CHAPTER 3

Genetic Engineering

Genetic engineering involves making changes to the DNA of a living thing. It is often in the news. There are stories about cloning (making exact genetic copies of) plants or animals, and even engineering new kinds of species. Usually this involves adding or replacing genes in eggs or developing embryos. Scientists have developed a range of tools to study genes and work with them.

Some uses of genetic engineering are controversial. Many people feel that putting genetic material from one living thing into another is wrong and could be dangerous, as genes from another species may have unexpected effects. In most countries there are strict rules controlling how genetic engineering is used, and what techniques are safe and acceptable.

Genetic engineering techniques are very useful in medicine. They are mainly used as a means of producing medically useful substances, including hormones (chemical 'messengers' that travel through the blood and have effects in various parts of the body) and antibodies (special proteins that help defend the body against disease).

Genetic enzymes

Enzymes play an important role in genetic engineering techniques. Enzymes are proteins that control chemical reactions in the body. They are catalysts: enzymes speed up chemical reactions without being used up themselves. Every

CUTTING EDGE
FACTS

Rearranging DNA molecules

Scientists use two types of enzymes, restriction enzymes and DNA ligases, as tools to rearrange DNA molecules. Restriction enzymes, produced by bacteria, detect the order of the base pairs on a strand of DNA and then select, or cut out, that specific area, leaving exposed 'sticky ends'. DNA ligases cause the exposed sticky ends of DNA molecules to reattach, forming an unbroken new strand of DNA.

process in the body is catalysed by an enzyme.

One of the first genetic enzymes to be discovered was DNA polymerase. This is the enzyme that makes two strands of DNA 'unzip'. In order for the DNA to copy itself, the two strands of the DNA molecule must 'unzip' from each other. Then, a new strand forms on each of the originals and they rejoin their complementary other half. With the help of DNA polymerase and other enzymes, it became possible for researchers to build their own DNA molecules in a test tube, or to make copies of a piece of DNA.

Scientists can also 'cut and paste' sections of DNA together using another useful group of enzymes called restriction enzymes. These enzymes act as biological 'knives' to cut, or isolate, smaller chunks of the DNA molecule. Most restriction enzymes cut one strand of the DNA in a specific place, and the other (complementary) strand in another place, several base pairs away. This leaves an uneven section of single-stranded DNA, known as a 'sticky end'. If a different piece of DNA is cut with the same restriction enzyme, then it too will have a sticky end. The two pieces of DNA can then be joined together using an enzyme called DNA ligase.

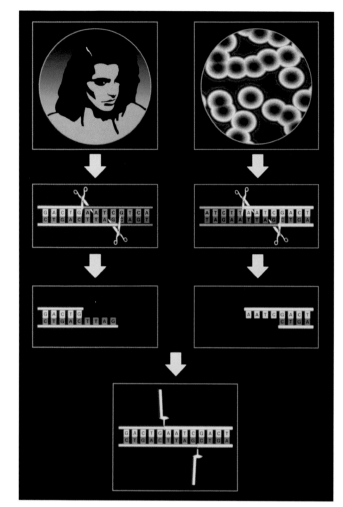

In this diagram, a restriction enzyme (scissors) is used to cut DNA in a human and in bacteria. The two cut pieces of DNA have 'sticky ends' that can be joined using the enzyme DNA ligase (shown as tubes of glue).

Protein factories

The discovery of genetic enzymes made genetic engineering possible. The most successful use of genetic engineering to date has been for making medically useful proteins. The genes of bacteria and other microbes have been turned into living 'factories' for producing proteins.

Finding the right gene

Genetically engineered microbes are most often used to make human proteins, which are slightly different from the same proteins in other animals. To do this, human genes have to be inserted into a microbe.

The first step in the process is to separate out the human gene that codes for the protein the scientists want to make. Finding a particular gene can take years of research, but once scientists know

A highly magnified microscope image of a bacterial plasmid. The highlighted section of the plasmid has been added by genetic engineering.

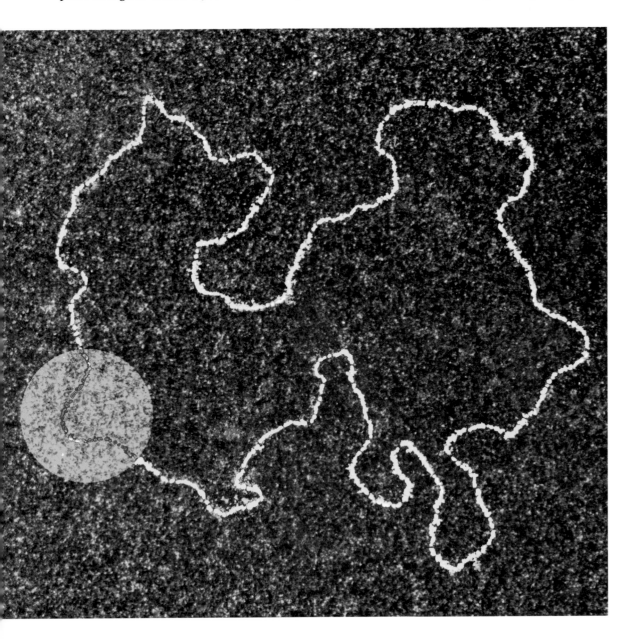

SCIENCE

Making human insulin

Insulin is a hormone – a 'messenger' protein that circulates in the blood and affects cells around the body. Insulin enables the body to absorb glucose (a form of sugar that is the main fuel of the body's cells) from the blood. People who have diabetes cannot make enough of their own insulin. They need regular insulin injections to stay healthy. In the past this insulin came from pigs, but pig insulin is not exactly the same as human insulin, so it sometimes caused problems. It was also expensive to produce.

Genetic engineering has made it possible to produce insulin using bacteria. Scientists have incorporated the gene for making the insulin protein into bacteria. Huge numbers of these bacteria are grown in large fermenters (apparatus used for growing micro-organisms), and they produce substantial amounts of human insulin.

where it is, they can separate it from other DNA using restriction enzymes. The result is a piece of DNA with 'sticky ends' that carries a specific human gene.

Using plasmids

Once the scientists have isolated the desired human gene, they need a way to transport it into a bacterial cell. One way of doing this is to use structures called plasmids – small, circular molecules of DNA that are found naturally in many bacteria. A plasmid usually contains a gene or genes that give the bacteria a useful characteristic. For instance, a plasmid could contain the gene or genes for making a restriction enzyme that would help defend it against some viruses. Bacteria can pass plasmids between themselves and copy the plasmids with the rest of their DNA when they divide.

Scientists use plasmids as a way of getting human DNA into bacteria. First they cut the plasmid using a restriction enzyme, turning it into a straight piece of DNA with 'sticky ends'. Next, they use another enzyme to join the piece of human DNA, which also has sticky ends, with the plasmid DNA. A plasmid containing DNA from different sources is known as a recombinant plasmid. It contains DNA that has been 'recombined'.

Once the recombinant plasmids have been made, researchers mix them with bacteria. The bacteria take up the plasmids, some of which contain the human gene, and begin to produce the required protein.

Medically useful products

The first medically useful protein to be genetically engineered was human insulin (see panel on page 23), which is used to treat diabetes. Genetically engineered human insulin was approved for use in humans in 1982. Since then, many other proteins have been made using a similar technique. For instance, proteins that help with blood clotting are produced to treat the genetic disorder haemophilia, in which the blood does not clot properly.

Another genetically engineered protein, erythropoietin, causes the body to produce red blood cells. This protein is used to treat anaemia, a condition in which there are too few red blood cells.

Several proteins that stimulate the immune system (the body's system of defending itself against disease) are also produced by genetic engineering. They are used as vaccines to prevent diseases such as viral hepatitis (a type of liver disease).

Yeasts and cell cultures

One problem with using plasmids to carry genetically engineered material into bacterial cells is that plasmids can only carry quite small chunks of DNA. Some genes, or groups of genes, are too large to be incorporated into a plasmid. Since the 1980s, yeasts (a more complex kind of microbe) and cell cultures (human or animal cells grown in the laboratory) have also been genetically modified and used as protein factories.

CUTTING EDGE   SCIENCE

What is a cell culture?
A cell culture is a colony (cluster) of cells from a human or animal that are grown in the laboratory. The cells are grown in carefully controlled conditions, either as single layers of cells on a glass or plastic surface or suspended (dispersed) in a liquid. One problem with many kinds of cell in culture is that they die after 50 to 100 divisions. However, a few kinds are 'immortal' – they continue dividing indefinitely. One of the most useful immortal cell types comes from the ovaries of Chinese hamsters.

A scientist purifies human insulin produced by genetic engineering. The insulin is produced by genetically engineered yeast. In this final stage of production, the insulin is separated out from the yeast cells in the large container in the foreground.

CHAPTER 4

Genetic Disorders

Medical researchers have made tremendous advances in the study of genetic disorders. From among the thousands of genes in the human genome, they have been able to pinpoint individual genes that cause genetic disorders, and the proteins that are produced by these genes.

How genetic disorders are passed on

We saw on page 19 that genetic disorders are usually caused by a change in just one gene. Most genes that cause genetic disorders are recessive, like the white flower colour in Mendel's pea plant experiments (see page 15). This means that only people who have two alleles (copies) of the 'faulty' gene actually show the illness. People with only one copy of the faulty gene also have a normal allele, and are not usually ill. Such people are, however, carriers – they can pass the disease on to their children.

People with genetic disorders often die in childhood, so they cannot pass on their genes to the next generation. But people who are carriers can have a normal life span and have children. So genes for genetic disorders are generally passed on from one generation to the next through carriers, rather than by people who actually get the disease.

Sickle cell syndrome

Most genetic disorders cause problems, but a few have positive side-effects. An example of this kind of disorder is sickle cell syndrome.

Sickle cell syndrome is a genetic disorder that affects haemoglobin, the protein that allows red blood cells (RBCs) to carry oxygen through the body. People who have sickle cell syndrome produce abnormal haemoglobin. The RBCs become sickle-shaped (crescent-shaped) and 'sticky'. This stickiness makes the sickle cells clump together to block blood vessels. The RBCs also break apart easily, which causes anaemia (low numbers of red cells).

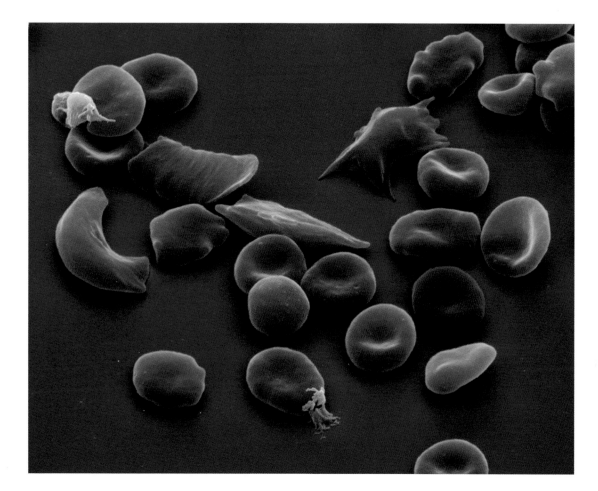

This micrograph shows normal red blood cells (disc-shaped) alongside the curved and distorted blood cells (pink) that are typical of sickle cell syndrome.

CUTTING EDGE — SCIENCE

Sickle cell genes

People who have two sickle cell alleles are usually very ill. Their heart is put under a lot of strain pushing the sticky sickle cells through their blood vessels, and they often die young of a heart attack. People who have only one sickle cell allele are only mildly affected by the disease.

People in tropical countries who carry the sickle cell gene develop a resistance to (immunity from) malaria. The sickle-shaped RBCs prevent the malaria parasites from reproducing in that person's body. Malaria is a major worldwide disease that causes at least one million deaths every year, so resistance to malaria is a great advantage.

This eight-cell embryo was produced by in vitro fertilization (fertilization in a test tube). It is being tested for genetic disorders before being implanted in the mother's womb.

Genetic testing

Once a gene for a hereditary disorder has been identified, it is relatively easy to test people to see if they are carriers of that gene. Genetic testing on babies, for example, is carried out on a drop of blood from the baby's heel (known as the heel prick test). People who might be carriers (for instance people who have relatives with the disorder) can have this test before they get married. If both partners are carriers of the disease, they need to think very carefully about having children, since there would be a one in four chance that their child would be born with the disease.

One genetic test developed in the 1990s promises to be useful for many people. About 1 in 200 people in the USA carries a gene that can cause cancer of the colon (the lower gut) in middle-aged people. In the early 1990s researchers found that this kind of cancer was caused by a faulty gene. People whose family have a history of colon cancer can be tested for the faulty gene. If they have the faulty gene, eating a special diet can greatly reduce the chances of getting colon cancer.

Genetic testing for a disease is not always helpful. Alzheimer's disease is a disorder that affects the brain. It causes forgetfulness at first, then sufferers may have problems speaking, understanding, reading or writing. Although it is a hereditary disorder, Alzheimer's does not usually affect people before they are 60. At present, there is no effective treatment or cure. It is possible to test for Alzheimer's disease, but a test may do more harm than good. A person cannot benefit from knowing that he or she is likely to get the disease, and the person may then have to live for years with the burden of this knowledge.

CUTTING EDGE MOMENTS

Genetic discrimination

To genetically discriminate against people means to treat them unfairly because of their genetic make-up. Research published in Australia 2005 suggests that genetic discrimination is already happening. In a study of 1,000 Australians who had taken genetic tests, 87 were found to have suffered some kind of discrimination as a result. One woman, for instance, who had been shown in tests to have a high risk of breast cancer, was refused health insurance for any kind of cancer.

Genetic weaknesses

Disorders caused by single faulty genes were once thought to be the only kind of genetic disorder. Today, many common disorders, such as heart disease and cancer, are known to be at least partly due to genetic causes. In these cases, people are said to have a 'genetic weakness' – they have particular alleles of one or more genes that make them more likely to develop a particular disease.

Having a genetic weakness does not mean that a person will definitely get a particular disease. Someone with a genetic weakness that makes him or her more likely to get heart disease, for instance, can greatly reduce the chances of getting this disease by exercising regularly and eating a healthy diet.

DNA microarrays

A new development in genetic testing, DNA microarrays (see panel), makes it possible to test for thousands of genes at the same time. DNA microarrays could be used to test for a wide range of genetic disorders or weaknesses. This kind of testing could offer tremendous benefits. People could be tested early in life, and doctors could then advise on a diet and lifestyle that would greatly reduce the risks from any genetic weaknesses they have. However, such widespread genetic testing could also lead to 'genetic

CUTTING EDGE SCIENCE

DNA chips

DNA microarrays, also known as DNA 'chips', are a fast and efficient way to do thousands of genetic tests at once. A DNA microarray is a flat plate that holds many different samples of DNA sequences, called probes, arranged in a regular grid. These probes are short pieces of DNA that link with 'targets' in the unknown sample to identify a particular genetic disorder.

When someone's DNA is tested using a DNA chip, a sample of their DNA is broken up into small pieces, and the pieces are 'labelled' with a fluorescent (glow-in-the-dark) dye. The DNA is then washed over the DNA microarray. If the person has a target section of DNA that matches one of the probes, that section binds to the DNA chip and shows up as a fluorescent dot. From the position of the dot on the plate, a doctor can identify the disorder.

discrimination' (see panel on page 29). Employers might refuse to employ someone who has a strong risk of developing a particular disorder. Insurance companies might also refuse to insure people who have a high 'genetic risk' of developing a serious illness.

A DNA microarray like this can carry out many genetic tests at once.

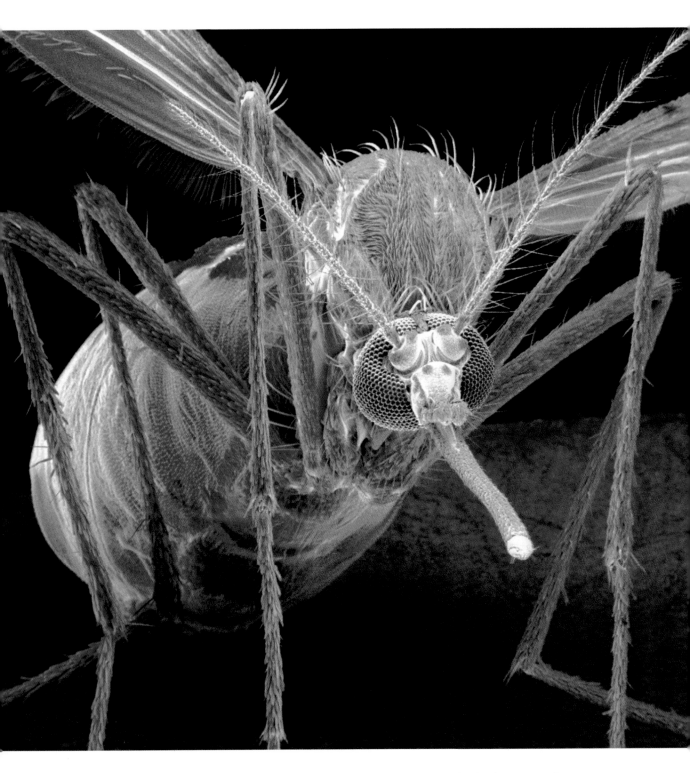

This mosquito is a carrier of a virus that causes the disease yellow fever in humans. Now scientists hope to use viruses to help cure people of disease.

Gene therapy

Gene therapy is an experimental medical technique that may eventually make it possible to cure people with genetic disorders. In gene therapy, doctors replace the 'faulty' gene or genes that cause a genetic disorder with a normal copy of the gene. With modern techniques it is fairly easy to make multiple copies of a particular gene. The challenge comes in incorporating the normal copy of the gene into the patient's DNA.

As we learned in Chapter 1, there are 100 trillion cells in an adult human. Inserting new DNA into every one of these cells would be an impossible task. In practice, most hereditary disorders affect particular areas of the body, and the new DNA need only be inserted in the cells in those areas. Even so, getting replacement genes into cells in the target area, and getting the genes to work, is extremely difficult.

Virus delivery

One way to get genes into cells is to use viruses. Viruses survive by getting into living cells and taking over the cell processes to make copies of themselves. This makes them ideal carriers for getting new genes into a patient's cells. The viruses that are used must be ones that are normally found in humans, because such viruses are less likely to be destroyed by the body's immune system. They also have to be genetically modified to stop them from causing disease.

Some kinds of viruses naturally attack particular parts of the body, and can be used to deliver the gene therapy to a specific area. Adenoviruses, for instance, are a group of viruses that attack the nose, throat, lungs or intestines, and they can be used to target the gene therapy on those areas.

CUTTING EDGE SCIENCE

DNA nanoballs
Another gene therapy method under development involves packing the genes into a tight ball and coating them with a protein layer. These particles, nicknamed 'DNA nanoballs', are small enough to pass into the nucleus of a cell. The nanoballs can be injected into the bloodstream, from where they are taken up into cells.

Non-viral carriers

There have been a number of cases in which people who have been given gene therapy using viruses have died or have become ill (see panel). Because of this, researchers are experimenting with new ways to get genes into the cell. One technique is to remove cells from the patient, add the new genes directly to the cells in the laboratory, then transfuse the genetically engineered cells back into the patient.

Another technique is to use small balls of lipids (natural oils or fats) known as liposomes. The replacement gene is placed inside these liposomes, which can join with a cell membrane and discharge the gene into the cell. Recently, microscopic liposomes have been developed that can get into the cell's nucleus. This is helpful because once a replacement gene gets into the nucleus, it is likely to survive and be reproduced along with the other genes, and its effects will last longer.

Problems and solutions

Gene therapy experiments on animals have been quite successful. In 2002, for instance, gene therapy was successfully used to correct sickle cell syndrome in mice. However, trials of gene therapies on humans have had very limited success, and there have been some worrying setbacks (see panel). These setbacks have made

CUTTING EDGE MOMENTS

Gene therapy failures

In 1999, 18-year-old Jesse Gelsinger, from Tucson, Arizona, USA, was taking part in a clinical trial (a large-scale test) of gene therapy at the University of Pennsylvania in Philadelphia, USA. Jesse had a genetic disorder that affected his liver and blood. The therapy was designed to cure the disease by inserting a new gene into the liver cells. It used a virus to transport the gene.

Within hours of being given the therapy, Jesse became very ill. His body's immune system began to run out of control. Despite the best efforts of the hospital doctors, Jesse died.

Since Jesse's death, several other people have been badly affected by gene therapy treatment. These problems have led to a complete rethink of research into gene therapy.

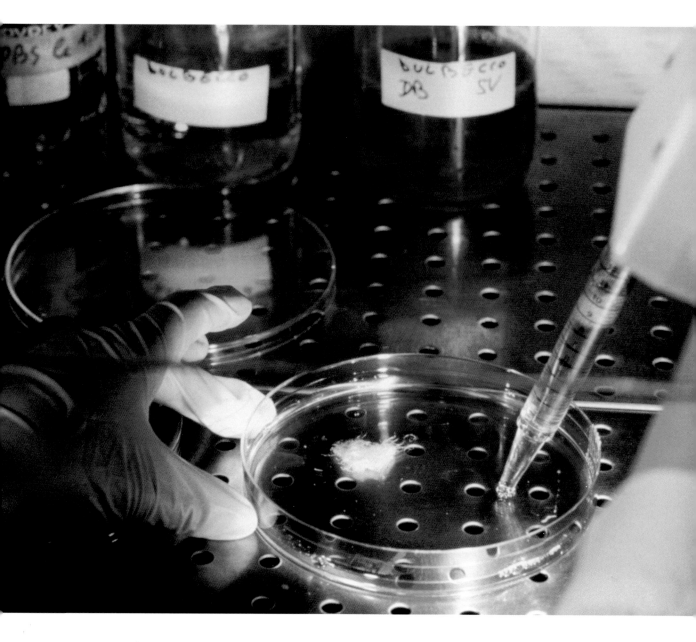

researchers cautious about using gene therapy. At present, all gene therapies on humans are experimental and are being tested for safety.

Although there are problems, gene therapy still promises great things. One new possibility involves persuading the cell's own DNA repair mechanisms to mend a faulty gene rather than replacing it altogether. Using this approach, there is no need to find a way of getting new genes into the cells.

A scientist prepares a gene therapy implant for insertion into a patient. The implant is made up of synthetic fibres mixed with genetically engineered cells.

CHAPTER 5

Cloning

A clone is a genetically identical copy of another animal or plant. There are quite a few kinds of clone found in nature. Identical twins are clones – they both come from the same fertilized egg. Some organisms, such as bacteria, yeasts and other microbes, are often clones of each other. They usually reproduce simply by dividing in two, then dividing again and again until there is a colony of billions of bacteria, all genetically identical. A few more complex animals are also clones. In aphids (greenfly) for instance, the female aphids produce thousands of young over the summer, all genetically identical to their mother.

Early clones

The idea of cloning was first proposed by the German scientist Hans Spemann in 1938. He suggested taking a body cell from an adult, taking out the nucleus, and putting this into an egg cell that has had

Identical twins are natural clones. They are formed when an embryo splits early in its development.

its nucleus removed. The first successful clones produced by this method were frogs. Two groups of researchers produced cloned frogs in 1962.

Scientists did not manage to clone a mammal until the 1980s. In 1984 the Danish scientist Steen Willadsen produced cloned sheep, and in 1985 he cloned cows. These clones were made by splitting a very early embryo into two. This process is now usually called 'twinning' rather than cloning. This is because the process involves making twins from a naturally fertilized egg, whereas other forms of cloning use adult body cells and unfertilized eggs.

Transgenic animals

The first scientists to clone a mammal from adult cells were actually looking for a way to reproduce transgenic animals reliably. Transgenic animals are animals that have been genetically engineered to contain a gene from another kind of animal. The scientists were hoping to produce transgenic farm animals that could produce human vaccines or other medical proteins in their milk. But when a transgenic animal breeds normally, only some of its engineered genes pass to some of its offspring. This occurs because, in normal breeding, only half the mother's genes pass to her offspring (see page 9). By using cloning, scientists hoped to overcome this problem, allowing them to quickly build up herds of transgenic animals.

Scientists have produced transgenic animals using other techniques besides cloning. The earliest method involved injecting extra genes into a newly fertilized egg using a very fine syringe. However, this technique proved unreliable: only between 1 and 5 percent of the animals produced were transgenic. This is probably because the injection process often damages the nucleus and the genes inside it, so the egg does not develop.

Another technique is to use a virus to carry extra genes into an egg cell, as in gene therapy. This technique has been used to produce transgenic mice for research purposes.

CUTTING EDGE   **SCIENCE**

Glowing green mice
In 2002, a group of transgenic mice was engineered to glow bright green! The mice received a gene for a fluorescent (glow-in-the-dark) protein produced by jellyfish. The idea of using the green colour was to show that the gene had been successfully incorporated into the mouse cells.

Three mothers

The first mammal cloned using DNA from a full-grown, adult animal was a sheep named Dolly. You could say that Dolly had three 'mothers'. Dolly's real mother was a white-faced breed of sheep. Dolly's DNA came from this mother. Scientists took an udder cell from the white-faced sheep and grew it in the laboratory under special conditions.

Next, they took an egg cell from the second of Dolly's 'mothers' – a black-faced sheep. Scientists removed the nucleus of this egg cell and inserted the nucleus from the udder cell. The combined cell and nucleus was given a tiny electric shock to make the two parts of the cell fuse (join) together. The electric shock also initiated cell division in the egg.

Once the scientists were sure that the egg was growing normally, they implanted it in the uterus of Dolly's third 'mother' – another black-faced female sheep. Dolly was born in July 1996. Her birth mother was a black-faced sheep, but Dolly's white face proved that she had the DNA of the white-faced sheep: Dolly was indeed a clone.

Worldwide excitement

Dolly's birth was not made public until 1997, when the researchers were fairly sure that she was developing normally. News of Dolly's arrival caused excitement around the world. There was talk of cloning beloved pets, or even successful people. With all the publicity surrounding Dolly, the original reason for her creation was

CUTTING EDGE   SCIENTISTS

Ian Wilmut (born 1944)

Ian Wilmut was the English scientist who led the research team that cloned Dolly the sheep. In 1973, while at Cambridge University, he created Frosty, the first calf to be grown from a frozen embryo. He moved to the Roslin Institute in Edinburgh, Scotland, in 1974. In early 1996 his research team cloned two sheep, Megan and Morag, from sheep embryo cells. Later that year, Wilmut's team cloned Dolly using DNA from an adult sheep. In 1997 his team produced a transgenic cloned sheep called Polly. Ian Wilmut is no longer cloning animals, but he continues to use genetic engineering for medical research.

frequently overlooked. The scientists who cloned Dolly were interested in making transgenic animals to produce vaccines and other useful human proteins. Scientists hoped that cloning would provide a way of producing large numbers of identical transgenic animals that could produce much-needed human proteins.

Dolly was the first successful clone, but she was not a transgenic animal. After the success of cloning Dolly, researchers went on to produce other cloned animals, including some transgenic animals that produced useful proteins in their milk.

There have been some successes, but as more clones are produced, the problems with the technique have also become clear. The success rate for this cloning technique is low: less than one clone in a hundred survives to birth. Also, there is evidence that even successful clones are damaged in some way during the cloning process, and age more quickly than normal animals. Dolly grew to adulthood and produced lambs, but she became seriously ill. Cloned animals have tended to die young. The reasons for the short lives of cloned animals are not understood at this time.

Dolly the sheep lived for seven years and gave birth to four lambs. In 2003, she was found to have a progressive lung disease, and the decision was taken to put her down.

Cloning success

Cloning has been shown to have problems, but the process is still a good way to produce transgenic animals. The transgenic animals can then be bred in the normal way. Genes are passed from parents to their offspring as Mendel originally described (see pages 14–17). As a result, some of the offspring do not receive the transgenic gene from their mother, while others do. A herd of transgenic animals can therefore be built up using normal breeding techniques.

Currently there are several herds of transgenic animals, each producing a different protein. One herd of goats, in Massachussetts, USA, produces a protein called antithrombin III, which reduces blood clotting. These transgenic proteins from milk will soon be helping patients and saving lives.

This photo shows part of the process of cloning a mouse by nuclear transfer. A mouse egg cell is held in place by a pipette (on the left). The egg nucleus has been removed, and a nucleus from an adult cell is being injected through a needle (on the right).

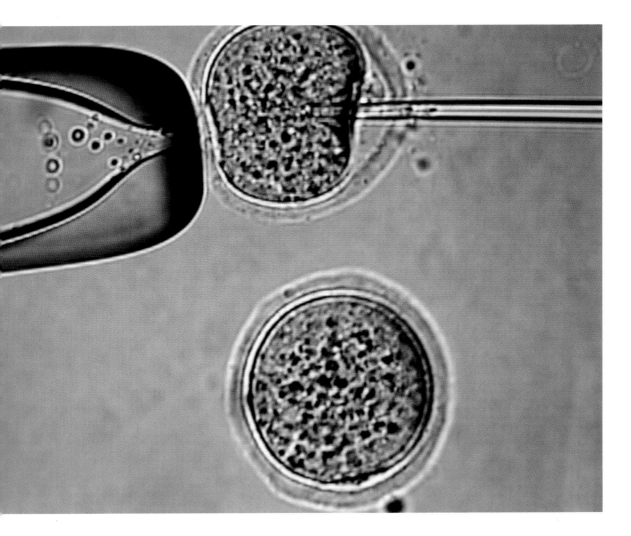

A cloned human?

It seems only a short step from cloning Dolly to cloning a human. However, most scientists say that cloning humans is far too risky at present. Judging from experience of animal cloning, a human baby cloned right now would have less than a 1 in 100 chance of survival. If a cloned human was born, it would perhaps grow to adulthood but it would have a short life, as Dolly did. With the techniques we have now, cloning humans is still in the realm of science fiction.

CUTTING EDGE — FACTS

Cloning timeline

1901	In Germany, Hans Spemann splits a two-cell newt embryo into two parts, resulting in the development of two complete larvae.
1952	In the USA, Robert Briggs and Thomas King clone frogs by taking the nuclei from early embryos and putting them into egg cells with the nucleus removed.
1975	British scientist J. Derek Bromhall clones a rabbit using a similar technique to that used for frogs.
1986	Danish scientist Steen Willadsen, working in Britain, finds that by using an electric shock he can fuse the nucleus of a sheep embryo with an enucleated egg cell (one that has had its nucleus removed). Using this technique, he clones a sheep. This is an advance from making clones by splitting an early embryo, and lays the groundwork for Dolly.
1996	In Scotland, Ian Wilmut and colleagues clone Dolly the sheep, the first mammal cloned using DNA from an adult animal.
1997	In the USA, Don Wolf and colleagues clone a rhesus monkey using the same techniques that were used for cloning Dolly. Ian Wilmut's team clone Polly the transgenic sheep.
1998	In the USA, Richard Seed and Lee Bo-yen claim to have cloned a human egg and grown it to the 4-cell stage. Claims are not proven.
1999	Japanese scientists Tenuhiko Wakayama and Ryuzo Yanagumachi clone a male mouse – the first male mammal to be cloned from adult cells.
2002	US Congress bans human cloning research.
2005	In South Korea, Woo-Suk Hwang and his team clone the first dog. Dogs have proved particularly hard to clone.

Xenotransplantation

The goats, sheep and cows being produced for their special milk are not the only transgenic animals that researchers are developing. Transgenic pigs are being developed so that their organs can be put into people. Transplantation of organs from one animal species to another is known as xenotransplantation.

Putting cells and organs from pigs into people sounds like a shocking idea. However, the technique could provide a solution for the world shortage of human organs for transplant. All over the world, seriously ill people are waiting for hearts, kidneys, livers, lungs and other organs because their own are not working properly. Unfortunately there are not enough donors to go round. In the USA, for instance, 70,000 people are on the waiting list for new organs.

The organs of a pig are about the same size as those of a human, so they could, in theory, be used for xenotransplants. Some experimental transplants have been made, but there is a stumbling block – organ rejection.

CUTTING EDGE   DEBATES

The xenotransplant debate

Although many people feel that xenotransplants could in time provide organs for transplant surgery, many others are strongly against this line of research. They argue that in the past 25 years there have been no successful xenotransplants, despite several attempts. The problems of rejection of non-human organs have not yet been solved. Even more worryingly, there is the possibility that a xenotranplant patient could be infected with a non-human virus. If this happened, it could potentially cause an epidemic.

'Me' or 'not me'

Rejection is a problem with all organ transplants. Our bodies are very good at recognizing what is part of us and what is not. Any material from another animal – even another human – sets off the body's immune system – its system for defending itself against disease.

White blood cells are one of the most important parts of the immune system. Some white blood cells can engulf substances that

This computer artwork shows the antigens (red) on the surface of a cell.

could be harmful to the body. Other white cells produce antibodies – proteins that recognize 'foreign' cells and destroy them.

Antibodies can detect cells that are 'not me' because the outside of every cell in the body has a chemical 'label' on it. These labels are called antigens and they are different in every individual. No two people have the same antigens, unless they are identical twins.

Transplant rejection

When a person has an organ transplant, the new organ has different antigens from the rest of the body. The immune system recognizes that the organ is 'not me'. The body's response is to reject the organ: the immune system attacks it and begins to break it down.

The more different an organ's antigens are from the body's own antigens, the more fiercely the immune system attacks it. Doctors looking for human organs to transplant must use organs with antigens that are as similar as possible to those of the patient. They then use drugs called immunosuppressants to keep the immune system from rejecting the transplanted organ.

Genetically engineered pigs

In addition to antigens, pig cells have other chemicals on their surface that cause severe immune reactions. Because of these chemicals, a normal pig organ would be rejected within hours of being transplanted into a human. To try and solve this problem, researchers have genetically engineered pigs that do not have these chemicals on their cells. This brings the prospect of using pig organs in xenotransplants one step nearer. However, it does not solve the problem of the antigens. Further genetic changes will need to be made before pig organs can be transplanted without rejection.

Problem viruses

Another possible problem with transplanting pig organs is pig viruses. Every species of animal has some viruses living inside their cells, actually incorporated into its DNA. If a pig organ is transplanted

CUTTING EDGE MOMENTS

Bridging the gap

In 1997, a British man called Robert Pennington nearly died of liver failure. Doctors wanted to carry out a liver transplant, but they could not find a suitable human liver. To keep Robert alive while they continued to look for a liver, surgeons diverted Robert's blood through the liver of a transgenic pig outside his body. The pig liver kept Robert alive for three days, after which a human liver was found for him. This was the first time an animal organ had been used in this way.

to a human, there are worries that the pig's viruses might become activated and destroy human body cells. Research suggests that this would not happen, but more research is needed to make sure.

Chimeras

Chimeras are another line of research that could lead to the production of animal organs that can be used for transplants. A chimera is an animal that is made up partly of one animal and partly of another. Chimeras that could be useful in transplant surgery are animals that include some human cells.

To make a chimera, human cells from culture (grown in a laboratory) are injected into the embryo of an animal inside its mother's womb. At this stage of life the embryo's immune system is not working, so the foreign cells are not rejected. The human cells grow and divide along with the embryo's other tissues. This results in patches of human tissue among the animal's normal body cells.

At present, researchers cannot control where the human cells in a chimera appear. Some day, it may be possible to produce chimeras that have one or more complete, working organs made up of human cells.

A chimera is made by combining cells from the early embryos of two different animals. This chimera was made by combining goat and sheep embryos. The adult animal has areas of sheep wool and areas of goat hair on its body.

CHAPTER 6

Stem Cells

The birth of Dolly the Sheep sparked a huge interest in cloning. Several laboratories claimed to be close to cloning a human, and this started a fierce public debate. Should we clone humans or not? Many people are against the idea. Some people with strong religious beliefs regard cloning as an offence against God, while many scientists think the risks involved in human cloning are far too great (see page 41).

However, most researchers working in the field of cloning are not interested in trying to produce cloned babies. They are interested in another type of cloning – therapeutic cloning. The aim of therapeutic cloning is to grow human embryos to the stage where they form a ball of cells with a cavity in the centre. This stage is known as a blastocyst. Inside a blastocyst there is a layer of very useful cells called an inner cell mass that contains embryonic stem cells. Many researchers think that stem cells could solve the problem of rejection in organ transplants and provide treatments for many other medical conditions.

CUTTING EDGE   **SCIENCE**

Immortal cells
Like Chinese hamster ovary cells (see page 24), stem cells seem to be immortal (when they are grown in the laboratory, they continue dividing indefinitely). However, human stem cells are slow to grow and difficult to look after.

What are stem cells?

Most cells in the human body are specialized. Nerve cells are cells with long, thin extensions that can carry electrical messages. Muscle cells are spindle-shaped cells that can contract (shorten). Red blood cells have no nucleus and are full of haemoglobin.

Specialized cells form through cell division, but once they specialize they lose the ability to divide. However, the tissues of the body must be able to grow, renew and repair themselves. So in each kind of tissue there are groups of stem cells. These stem cells are the body's biological repair kit. They have not lost the ability to divide. They provide a constant supply of specialized cells, such as muscle or blood cells, to replace others that are damaged or have died.

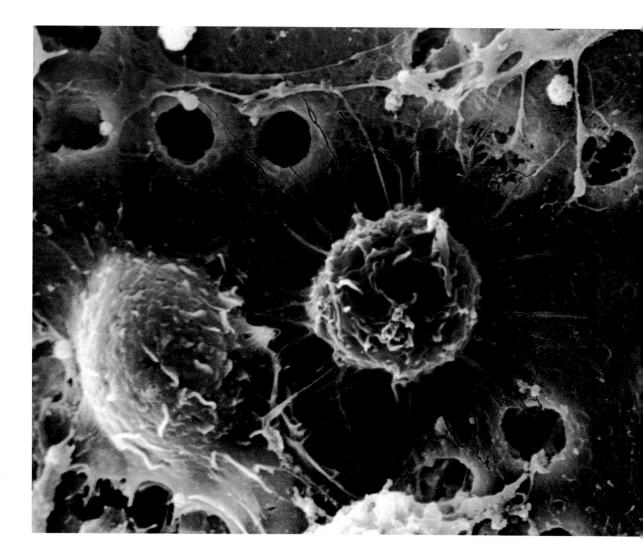

In this microscope image, the purple cell on the right is a bone marrow stem cell.

Adults have many different kinds of stem cells, each of which can make one or a few kinds of specialized cell. Stem cells in muscle tissue make muscle cells, for instance, while stem cells in the bone marrow can make red and white blood cells and platelets (small, disc-like cell fragments that circulate in the blood and are important for blood clotting).

A donor kidney is prepared prior to a transplant operation. Transplanting a kidney is a fairly simple operation, but there is a serious shortage of kidney donors. Researchers hope that progress in stem cell research will make it possible to grow new kidneys from stem cells.

Embryonic stem cells

Stem cells from embryos are different from adult stem cells. Adult stem cells can divide and specialize into one or a few kinds of tissue. However, embryonic stem cells can become any kind of body cell or tissue. Researchers are interested in embryonic stem cells because they have enormous medical potential. For instance, they could be used to regrow damaged nerves in people who are paralysed because of an injury to their spinal cord. Or stem cells could be used to produce insulin in people with diabetes (see page 23).

In time, stem cells could be used to grow complete new organs that could be used in transplant surgery. However, as with organs donated for transplant surgery, there is the problem of rejection (see pages 42–43). Much of current genetic research is focused on solving this problem.

Cloning stem cells

The best way to avoid the rejection of stem cells would be to use stem cells with the same genetic make-up as the patient.

Researchers have realized that it might be possible to do this using the techniques used to clone Dolly and other animals. If a nucleus from one of the patient's own cells could be inserted into a human egg cell, this egg could then be allowed to grow until embryonic stem cells were formed. The stem cells could then be grown into new tissues or organs. Since the stem cells would have the same DNA as the patient, there would be no problems of rejection, because their surface antigens would be the same as those of other body cells.

Successes and setbacks

Although therapeutic cloning is straightforward in theory, researchers are still a long way from being able to clone stem cells. However, there has been some progress. In November 2001, a group of scientists in Massachusetts, USA, took an egg cell from a woman's ovary and removed its nucleus. They then inserted the nucleus from an adult body cell. The resulting combination began to divide, but the egg cell did not divide for long enough to produce stem cells. It grew only to the six-cell stage, then stopped growing.

In 2004, South Korean researchers reported success in creating human stem cells using the method used by the Massachusetts scientists. However, an investigation in 2006 showed that these research results were false (see panel on page 51). This was a serious setback for stem cell research.

CUTTING EDGE **SCIENCE**

Stem cell therapy

Recent work has suggested that a patient's own stem cells can be used to treat some kinds of illness. In one life-threatening disorder called lupus, a fault in the body's immune system causes it to attack its own body tissues. A new treatment for lupus involves first removing a sample of stem cells from the patient's bone marrow and storing them. Bone marrow stem cells are responsible for producing the white blood cells that are central to the body's immune system. Once the bone marrow stem cells have been removed, a mixture of strong drugs is used to destroy the patient's faulty immune system. The bone marrow stem cells are then put back in the body with the hope that they will rebuild the patient's immune system.

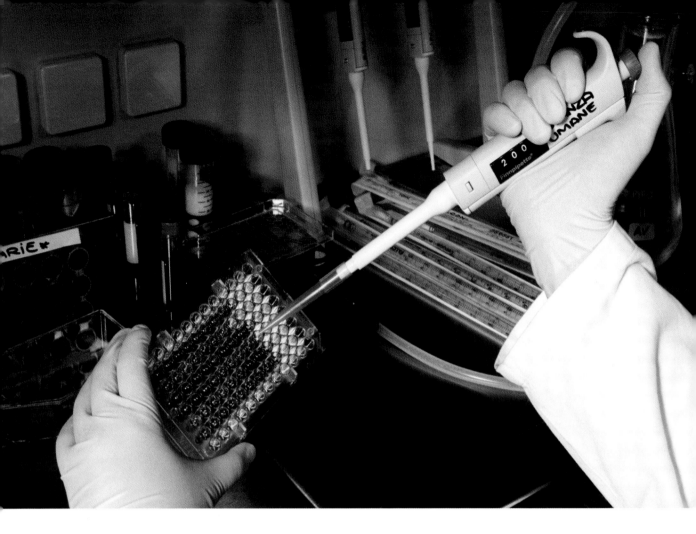

Stem cell lines

Another way of avoiding the rejection of stem cells would be to develop a number of different stem cell types (known as 'cell lines'). Researchers are aiming to develop about 1,000 or so genetically different cell lines, and keep each line growing in cell culture. Because stem cells are 'immortal' (see panel on page 46), each cell line could be kept dividing indefinitely in the laboratory. With this number of cell lines, it should be possible to find one that is a close genetic match for any patient needing new tissues or organs. Each type would not be an exact match to an individual patient, but the match would be close enough to allow the stem cells to be used (in combination with drugs that suppress the immune system) without the body rejecting them.

Although stem cells cannot yet be grown from unfertilized eggs by replacing the nucleus, there is another technique that does work. Doctors take two unfertilized eggs from the same woman, and take the genetic material from one egg and add it to the other. The egg

A researcher experiments on stem cells. Stem cells can be stimulated to develop into any kind of body tissue.

now has double its normal number of genes – but remember that gametes have only half the number of genes of a normal cell. So an unfertilized egg with double the number of genes has the correct number to develop normally. As in other kinds of cloning, the doctors can start the modified egg cell dividing using a tiny electric shock.

Ethical issues

Many researchers are convinced that research involving embryonic stem cells is justified because it can provide us with great medical benefits. Large numbers of people are opposed to this work because it involves tampering with, and destroying, embryos that have the potential to develop into human beings. There is also the fear that once therapeutic cloning has been perfected, it will lead to the cloning of human babies. As discussed on page 46, many people have practical and ethical objections to human cloning.

For these reasons, the USA does not allow government-funded research into therapeutic cloning. Some scientists in the USA are therefore taking another approach to stem cell research, They are isolating different kinds of adult stem cells, then trying to find ways of genetically engineering these cells to be medically useful. Scientists have had some success in using a patient's own stem cells (see panel on page 49), but genetically modified adult stem cells have not been used medically.

CUTTING EDGE   MOMENTS

Faking the results

In January 2006, a public enquiry (investigation) into the work of South Korean scientist Woo-Suk Hwang found that he had faked the results of two stem cell studies. In these studies he claimed to have inserted DNA from adults into human egg cells, grown the eggs to blastocyst stage and harvested the stem cells. The enquiry found that the photographs and other evidence for this research were false. Why did a respected scientist decide to falsify results? The public enquiry found that Hwang's earlier achievement of cloning the first dog was authentic, so he was obviously capable of high-quality research work. The most likely explanation is that Hwang falsified his results in order to maintain his high status in Korea and to ensure that his research continued to receive funding.

CHAPTER 7

Combating Aging

Most people would like to live a long and healthy life. Today, people in the West generally live longer than they did in the past, mainly due to improvements in public health. However, many elderly people suffer from illnesses and pain. Genetics offers the possibility of making our old age healthier. It may even allow us to live longer.

Evolution and aging

There is some evidence to suggest that we get old because of natural selection. Natural selection is often called 'survival of the fittest'. It is the process by which the individuals best suited to a particular environment survive to reproduce and pass on their genes. Genes that cause illness are weeded out because, as we saw on page 26, people who have genetic disorders are less likely to survive and reproduce. However, once we have reproduced and brought up children, natural selection does not operate – keeping fit and strong is no longer an advantage. It may therefore be due to natural selection that we age and die when we do.

There is strong evidence to suggest that fitness really does help people survive. People who eat well and keep fit throughout their lives are likely to remain healthy into their old age.

Longevity genes

There is some evidence from experiments with fruit flies to suggest that natural selection has an effect on aging. Scientists at the University of California Irvine found that they could make flies live longer by delaying the age when they reproduced.

From experiments on fruit flies and research using other animals, genetic researchers have identified a number of 'longevity genes' that are connected with living longer. Many of these genes help an animal to combat stresses from the environment, such as harmful chemicals or radiation that can cause mutations. Longevity genes also affect the body's defences and its genetic repair mechanisms. In the case of the long-lived fruit flies, the gene that gave longevity (named the Methuselah gene) acted by stopping cells from self-destructing under stress.

Perhaps the most promising longevity gene is called SIR2. This gene was originally found in yeasts and worms, but humans have a version, too. SIR2 is more active when the body is under stress. One of its effects may be to stop cells from self-destructing when they become stressed. Over time, cell destruction causes aging.

CUTTING EDGE   FACTS

Longevity genes

Several genes that can affect life span are listed in the table below.

Gene or protein	Found in	Increase in life span	Increase or decrease in gene produces increased life span?	Effects of gene
SIR2	Yeast, worm, fly	30 percent	Increase	Stops cells from self-destructing under stress
daf-2	Worm, fly, mouse	100 percent (live twice as long)	Decrease	Growth and breakdown of food for energy
Growth hormone	Mouse, rat	7 to 150 percent, depending on levels of hormone	Decrease	Regulates body size
Catalase (CAT)	Mouse	20 percent	Increase	Reduces free radicals (see pages 54–55)
Klotho	Mouse	18 to 31 percent	Increase	Regulates some hormones and parts of the immune system
Methuselah (CD97)	Fly	35 percent	Decrease	Stops cells from self-destructing under stress and improves communication between nerve cells

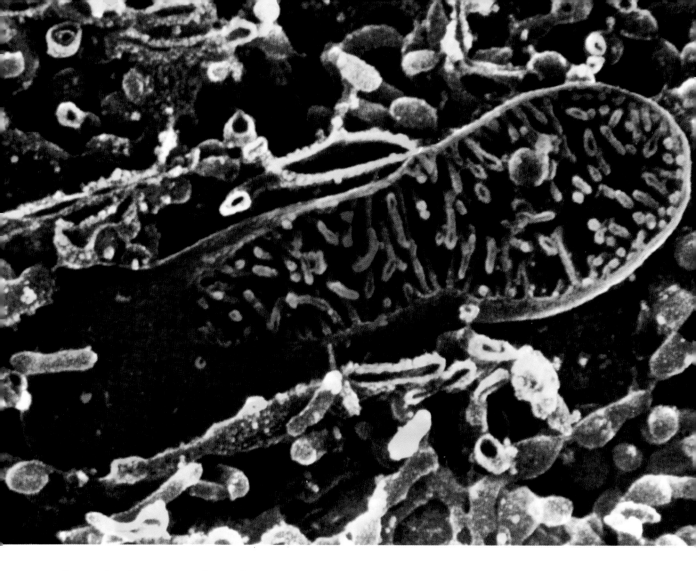

Genes in the energy factories

Another promising line of research into aging is concerned with substances called free radicals. These are destructive chemicals that can damage DNA, proteins or other large, complex molecules that are found in cells. Fruit flies that have been bred with supercharged defences against free radicals live significantly longer than normal.

Recent research on mice suggests that the main effects of free radicals are in mitochondria. Mitochondria are the energy factories of cells. They are the places where nutrients from food are broken down to release energy that the body can use to keep itself going. The process requires oxygen, and any mistakes or interruptions can cause free radicals to form.

Although 99 percent of DNA is in the nucleus of a cell, there is also a small amount in mitochondria. Mitochondrial DNA codes for proteins involved in energy production. The free radicals that

A microscope image of a mitochondrion from a cell in the intestines. Doctors think that damage to DNA in the mitochondria may be a major cause of aging.

sometimes form during energy production can damage mitochondrial DNA. Our cells have defences to protect mitochondrial DNA, but it is still more likely to be damaged than the genetic material in the nucleus. Mitochondria with damaged DNA do not work properly. When enough mitochondria are damaged, cells begin to die, and this causes aging.

Researchers are looking at ways of improving the life span of mitochondria by boosting our defences against free radicals. Compounds such as vitamin E, known as antioxidants, occur naturally in the body. These compounds can change free radicals and make them harmless. As yet, however, scientists do not know how to increase the activity of antioxidants in the places where they are needed.

Do we want to live longer?

People in developed countries already live longer, healthier lives than in the past. If this trend continues, humans will face some new challenges. There are already over 6 billion people in the world. If people live longer, this will cause the population to rise still further. How would we feed and house everyone? If people live longer, will they also be more healthy in old age? If not, the medical costs for the large numbers of older people will become very high. Finally, if people live longer, when should they retire? It will no longer be possible for people to retire at the traditional ages of 60 or 65, because it will cost too much to pay pensions to people for the 30 or 40 years of life left to them after they retire.

CUTTING EDGE   SCIENCE

Guaranteed to lengthen life

One method of prolonging life has been known for over 70 years and has been tested in several animal species. If animals are fed 30 to 40 percent less than their normal diet throughout their lives, they live longer and are healthier. A starvation diet seems to give protection against many illnesses as well as prolonging life. However, the experiment has not been tested over the long term in humans – not many people want to starve themselves all their lives in the hope of living longer!

CHAPTER 8

The Future

There have been some remarkable advances in the field of genetics over the past few decades. The sequence of bases along the whole human genome is known, and thousands of genes have been identified. Geneticists can extract genes from human DNA and make many copies of them. They can splice genes into microbes or into cell cultures to make protein factories. They can take all the genes from one animal and put them in an egg cell and grow them.

To date, medical genetics has achieved only a limited amount. We understand the causes of thousands of genetic disorders, and there are tests for many of these disorders. We can manufacture many medically useful human proteins by genetic engineering. Yet genetics is still in its infancy. We are on the verge of a genetic revolution that could transform medicine.

CUTTING EDGE SCIENCE

What about RNA?
Until recently, genetic scientists focused exclusively on those parts of human DNA that code for proteins – the genes. However, research carried out since the 1990s has shown that large sections of DNA that do not contain any genes, code for various kinds of RNA (see page 11) that are not involved in producing protein. There is growing evidence that these different kinds of RNA have important roles in the cell. Some kinds of RNA, like enzymes, can control processes within the cell. Other RNAs can shut down or start up genes. It could be that some genetic disorders are related to RNA rather than to protein. More importantly, it might be possible to use RNA to treat some disorders, for instance by shutting down a faulty gene.

An amazing repair kit

Stem cells are likely to be at the forefront of this revolution. Techniques for incorporating a patient's DNA into stem cells have to be perfected, and researchers need to find out how to control the ways that stem cells develop. Once these problems are overcome, doctors will have an enormously powerful body repair kit. Stem cells could be grown into new nerves, muscles, bones or other tissues to repair damage caused by accidents or illness.

Researchers have already successfully grown organs from patients' own cells on frameworks of protein fibres. It may soon be possible to use this technique to grow organs from stem cells. We might even be able to print new organs! Modified inkjet printers can already be used to lay down layers of living cells in a gel that becomes solid when warmed. If this technology was used with stem cells, organ printing might become a reality.

The coloured bands on this computer screen show some of the three billion base pairs that make up the genetic code of human DNA. Each of the coloured bands represents the position of one of the four nucleotide bases that form the genetic code. As we learn more about what each part of our DNA does, our ability to use genetics in medicine will improve.

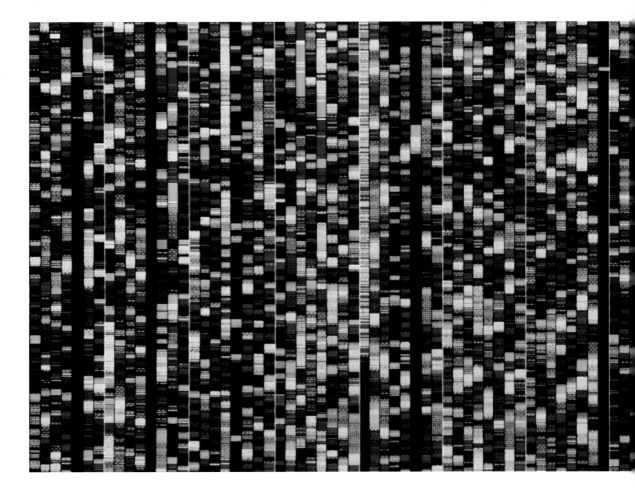

Gene therapy

We do not yet have the tools to deliver replacement genes to parts of the body where they are needed, and make them work. But once we can do these things, gene therapy could also revolutionize medicine. It could offer treatments or even cures for a whole range of genetic disorders, including Alzheimer's disease, sickle cell syndrome, Down's syndrome and many others.

A computer-generated image showing cloned babies. In reality, genetic researchers cannot yet clone humans. But one day we may be able to choose some of the characteristics of our children, and possibly clone them.

Genetic smart cards

DNA microarrays have already speeded up genetic testing enormously, and in the near future it may be possible to test the whole of our DNA at birth. Knowledge of genetic disorders and weaknesses would make it possible for us to improve our health. Doctors could advise us on how to live to avoid the diseases that we are at risk from.

The whole sequence of our DNA could be saved on a smart card that we could carry around. If we become ill or are injured, the smart card will have the information to tailor treatment to fit each individual (see panel). Full genetic testing could also be used to identify and correct genetic disorders before a baby is born.

CUTTING EDGE SCIENCE

Tailor-made treatment

The more we know about an individual's genome, the more doctors can tailor treatment for any illness to match the individual. Heart disease, for instance, has many different forms. It can be caused by lack of exercise and poor diet, for instance, but it can also be one of several genetic disorders. Although doctors can easily diagnose heart disease, finding the underlying cause is not so straightforward. If a doctor knows that a patient has a specific gene allele, the doctor can offer treatment targeted to that form of the disease.

Controlling genetics

Along with the benefits of medical genetics will come some tough decisions. Is it acceptable to obtain stem cells by breaking open embryos that could grow into humans? Should we use other animals to carry out genetic experiments that may sometimes cause those animals harm? We already have problems with criminals stealing personal information – how can we protect an individual's genetic information? Should we allow cloning of humans, or is this playing at God? As genetics finds more uses in medicine, society will have to make decisions about these issues.

Glossary

allele A particular version of a gene.

amino acids The raw materials that are joined together to make a protein.

antibody A protein produced by white blood vessels that can destroy disease-causing microbes.

antigen A microbe, a harmful chemical or other substance that stimulates the immune system to produce antibodies.

bacteria Microscopic, primitive single-celled living things in which the DNA is loose in the cell rather than in a nucleus.

catalyst A substance that speeds up a chemical reaction but is not used up itself in the reaction.

cell culture Human or other animal cells that are grown in a laboratory.

chromosome One of 23 long structures in the cell nucleus. Each chromosome is a single DNA molecule.

clone An exact genetic copy of another living thing. Identical twins are clones.

DNA (deoxyribonucleic acid) The genetic material, which contains all the information needed to make a living thing.

dominant trait The (usually) physical characteristic displayed in an offspring caused by the inheritance of a gene carried by only one parent (see recessive trait).

embryo A very young human or animal in the early stages of development inside the uterus.

enzymes Proteins found in living things, which speed up the chemical reactions that are essential to life.

evolution The gradual changes over time in groups of living things.

fermenter A large container that holds bacteria or other microbes, kept under ideal conditions for growth and used for large-scale production of proteins from genetically modified microbes.

fluorescent A material that glows in the dark.

gamete The eggs or sperm cells of an animal.

gene A section of DNA that carries the information to produce a protein or a group of proteins.

gene therapy Treatment for a genetic disorder that involves giving the patient a working copy of the damaged gene that is causing the disorder.

genetic disorder A disease or illness caused by a gene that does not work properly or is different from normal.

genetic engineering Making changes to the DNA of an animal or plant.

genetics The study of how we inherit characteristics and pass them on.

genome All the genes of a particular living organism.

genotype The underlying genetic make-up behind a certain characteristic.

haemophilia A genetic disorder of the blood in which the blood does not clot properly.

hormone A chemical 'messenger' that travels through the blood to affect cells around the body.

immune system The body's defence system against disease and injury.

mammal A warm-blooded animal, usually hairy or furry, that feeds its young on breast milk.

messenger RNA A material similar to DNA, used to copy genetic information from DNA and carry it to the ribosomes.

mutation A spontaneous change in the sequence of bases along a DNA molecule, produced by radiation, chemicals or some other cause.

natural selection The process by which those individuals most suited to an environment survive and reproduce, while other individuals do not.

nucleotide One of the subunits that make up DNA.

nucleus A round structure found inside living cells. The nucleus is the control centre of a cell.

phenotype The physical characteristics of an individual that are controlled by their genes.

platelets Small, disc-like cell fragments that circulate in the blood and are important for blood clotting.

proteins An important group of substances that make up living structures such as skin, hair and muscle and also control processes inside cells.

recessive trait A (usually) physical characteristic that does not appear in offspring unless it is inherited within genes from both parents (see dominant trait).

rejection When the body's immune system attacks a transplanted organ and the organ stops working.

ribosome A small structure in the cell that is the site for protein production.

RNA (ribonucleic acid) A substance similar to DNA that carries genetic information around the cell.

sequencing In genetics, determining the order of bases along a DNA molecule.

stem cells Undifferentiated (non-specialized) cells that have the potential to divide and develop into many different kinds of cell.

transgenic animal An animal that has been genetically modified to carry genes from a human or another organism.

ultraviolet A form of light that humans cannot see, which is close to blue and violet light.

vaccine A substance that is given to a person to stimulate their immune system to produce antibodies against a disease.

virus A very simple living thing, made from DNA or RNA and protein, which reproduces by invading living cells and using them to make copies of itself.

xenotransplantation Transplanting an organ from one species of animal into another.

yeast A tiny, single-celled microbe that is a type of fungus. Yeasts are used for making bread, beer and wine. They can also cause infections.

Further Information

BOOKS

Genes and DNA by Richard Walker (Kingfisher Books, 2003)

Gregor Mendel: Genetics Pioneer by Della Yannuzzi (Franklin Watts, 2004)

History of Medicine: Medicine in the Twentieth Century by Alex Woolf (Wayland, 2006)

Tomorrow's Science: Genetic Engineering by Anne Rooney (Chrysalis Children's Books, 2003)

21st Century Citizen: Genetic Engineering by Paul Dowswell (Franklin Watts, 2004)

21st Century Debates: Genetics by Paul Dowswell (Wayland, 2000)

WEBSITES

www.dnaftb.org/dnaftb/
DNA from the Beginning: an excellent, easy to read website covering most areas of genetics using animations.

library.thinkquest.org/19697/index.htm
A site made by students about genetic engineering and cloning. It includes some simple games and quizzes.

www.sciencemuseum.org.uk/antenna/ dolly/index.asp
Dolly the sheep, 1996–2003: an overview of Dolly's life from the Science Museum in London.

www.roslin.ac.uk/public/cloning.html
Cloning: a discussion on cloning from the Roslin Institute website (the place where Dolly the sheep was cloned).

www.ncbi.nlm.nih.gov/books/bv.fcgi? call = bv.View..ShowSection&rid = gnd. preface.91
Genes and Disease: a list of all the known genetic diseases, and the genes that cause them, shown chromosome by chromosome.

www.ornl.gov/sci/techresources/Human_ Genome/medicine/medicine.shtml
Medicine and the New Genetics: medical genetics information from the Human Genome Project.

Index

Index (continued)

hormones 20, 23, 53, 60
Human Genome Project 18

identical twins **36**, 36, 43
immune system 24, 33, 34, 42, 44, 45, 49, 53, 60
immunosuppressants 44, 50
insulin 23, 24, **25**, 48
in vitro fertilization **28**

liposomes 34
longevity 5, 52–55
longevity genes 53

malaria 28
Mendel, Gregor 14–16, **15**, 26, 40
messenger RNA 11, 61
metabolism 11
mitochondria 54, **54**, 55
mitochondrial DNA 54–55
molecules 9, 54
mutations 19, 53, 61

natural selection 52, 61
nucleotides 6, 7, 61
nucleus 4, 6, 8, 11, 16, 33, 34, 36, 37, 38, **40**, 41,
    46, 49, 54, 55, 61

organ transplantation 4, 42, 44–45, 46, 48–49, **48**,
    50, 57

phenotype 13, 15, 18, 61
pigments 12
plasmids **22**, 23, 24
proteins 11, 12, 13, 14, 18, 19, 20, 21, 22, 23, 24,
    26, 33, 37, 39, 40, 43, 54, 56, 57, 61

recessive traits 15, 26, 61
red blood cells 6, 14, 19, 24, 26, 27, 46
rejection 42–44, 45, 46, 48–49, 50, 61
reproduction 8, 9, 36, 52
restriction enzymes 20, 21, **21**, 23
ribosomes 11, 61
RNA 11, 56, 61

sickle cell syndrome 19, 26–28, **27**, 58
Spemann, Hans 36, 41
sperm cells 8, **8**, 9
stem cells 46–51, **47**, 57, 59, 61

therapeutic cloning 46–49, 51
transgenic animals 37, 38, 39, 40, 61

vaccines 24, 37, 39, 61
viruses 23, 33, 34, 37, 42, 44–45, 61

Watson, James **10**, 11
white blood cells 42–43, 49
Willadsen, Steen 37, 41
Wilmut, Ian 38, 41

xenotransplantation 42, 44, 61

yeasts 24, **25**, 36, 53, 61